GEO

THE TRUMPET

THE TRUMPET

An Illustrated
Step-by-Step
Instructional Guide

Frank Cappelli

ELDORADO INK

Eldorado Ink
PO Box 100097
Pittsburgh, PA 15233
www.eldoradoink.com

First printing

1 3 5 7 9 8 6 4 2

Library of Congress Cataloging-in-Publication Data

   Cappelli, Frank.
    The trumpet / Frank Cappelli.
      p. cm. — (Learn to play)
    Includes bibliographical references (p.   ) and index.
    ISBN-13: 978-1-932904-16-1
    ISBN-10: 1-932904-16-6
    1. Trumpet—Methods. I. Title.
    MT442.C26 2007
    788.9'2193—dc22

                  2006036436

Acknowledgements

The author would like to thank all of those who provided instruments to be used in the photographs of this book, particularly Volkwein's Music of Pittsburgh (800-553-8742; www.volkweins.com).

TABLE OF CONTENTS

Part Four: Songs and Exercises

Clarinet
Flute
Guitar
Piano
Trumpet
Violin

INTRODUCTION

The early horns were animal horns or conch shells. If you blow into these simple shapes, it makes a tone, often one that carries a good distance. Based on these naturally occurring instruments, humans eventually fashioned horns of their own. There is archeological evidence that metal trumpets were used as far back as Ancient Egypt, but they were not musical instruments at that time. Originally, the trumpet was used as a battle call. It was a communication device used to coordinate troops.

The trumpet of thousands of years ago was a long, slender tube with a flare at the end. It had a mouthpiece of sorts at one end and a bell at the other and could be many feet long. It did not look much like the trumpet of today. There were no valves or complicated wound tubing. An ancient trumpet could only make a few tones based on the inherent harmonics within the tube and bell, but since no one thought of this as a musical instrument, it wasn't considered a limitation at the time. People were more concerned with trying to make the instruments louder.

Simple trumpets existed in early Chinese, Egyptian, Mayan, and Incan civilizations. Even the primitive tribes who lived in the Amazon rainforests of Brazil had a horn instrument.

The Romans developed a round trumpet called a cornu that looped down and around the back, placing the bell over the player's shoulder. But even this design was large and unwieldy. It wasn't until the 1500s that metalworkers found a way to bend the long tube of metal in a compact way. They called the technique folding. The new trumpet was easier to hold and carry, but it was still used as a communication device.

The bugle is a perfect example of the kind of instrument created using the folding technique. A short time later, crooks were invented. Crooks were small additional lengths of tube that would attach to the trumpet and allow it to play tones in a different key. With this technological advancement, the trumpet became a real musical instrument, and composers started to write music that included a trumpet part.

Initially, it was not uncommon in bands and orchestras for one person to play just the low notes while another trumpeter played the higher notes, simply because switching crooks would have taken too long. But this problem was solved in 1814 with the addition of valves. These allowed the trumpet to play all the notes in the scale by opening and closing various lengths of tubing. The trumpet of 1814 is similar to the instrument of today.

PART ONE: THE TRUMPET BASICS

This book is for the beginning trumpet player. Give yourself time and always look for new ways to make yourself better. When you get the chance, play with other musicians. You will learn from them as they will learn from you.

You will find that the trumpet is a great instrument. Anyone can play the trumpet; as with most other things in life, it all depends on how much time you want to put into it. It is my hope that with this fresh approach to learning the trumpet, you will come to enjoy practicing and playing. Whether you are a true beginner, have a bit of musical training, or are a skilled musician on another instrument, our carefully developed approach can help anyone succeed and continue to enjoy playing the trumpet.

Remember, to become a trumpet player you need to work hard and practice. Listen to some of your favorite songs and see if you can pick out notes or melodies that you can play on your own. Even if you can't play all of the notes, this kind of practicing will improve your skill.

You will experience exhilaration and frustration as you learn to understand and master the trumpet. Hopefully the way we have structured this book will make your experience learning the trumpet as stress free as possible. The instructions, diagrams, and illustrations will help you through everything from the purchase of a trumpet to playing your first songs.

1. Buying a Trumpet

Go to a music store and ask to hold and play the trumpets. Ask questions about the instruments. Remember, most people who work in a music store are musicians, and they love to talk about music. Here are some questions that you should ask:

Do you have different models?
What is the difference between the different models?
May I try it out?
What makes this trumpet so good?
Should I buy a used trumpet?
Can I buy a trumpet online?
Does the trumpet come with any guarantee?

As you're looking over the instrument, check it carefully for dings or problems with the finish. Shake the instrument slightly—if you hear a rattle, the valves may be too loose. Good brands for beginners include Yamaha, King, Getzen, and Conn, to name a few.

One of the first things to consider is whether you'd like to play a trumpet or a cornet. The cornet is just a little bit smaller than a trumpet, but the fingering is the same. If you are planning on playing in a band, ask your band director if he would prefer one instrument over the other. If there's no preference, then choose whichever one feels good to you and will encourage you to play often.

HELPFUL TIP:
Buying a trumpet can be expensive. If you're not sure whether you want to invest the money in a good instrument before you have learned how to play it, ask the salesperson whether his or her store has a rental program.

2. The Parts of the Trumpet

Every trumpet is made up of a number of separate parts. These include the mouthpiece, leadpipe and tubing, valve slides, pistons, valve casings, finger hook, tuning slide, and bell.

The mouthpiece is the part of the trumpet that touches your lips. The way you place your lips against the trumpet will give you your sound. There are five parts to the mouthpiece.

1. The rim: The part that touches your lips.
2. The cup: Beginners should use a medium cup. Professionals use a small cup to make it easier to play higher notes or a large cup to help to play lower notes. But, beginners should use a medium cup.
3. The throat: The diameter of the hole in the mouthpiece.
4. The backbore: This key piece is hidden inside the mouthpiece; its length and diameter affect the trumpet's sound.
5. The shank: This is the part that connects the mouthpiece to the trumpet's tubing.

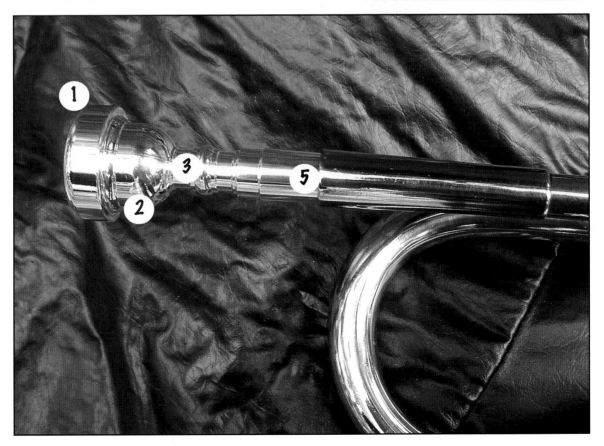

Trumpet mouthpieces can vary greatly in size. Here are some examples:

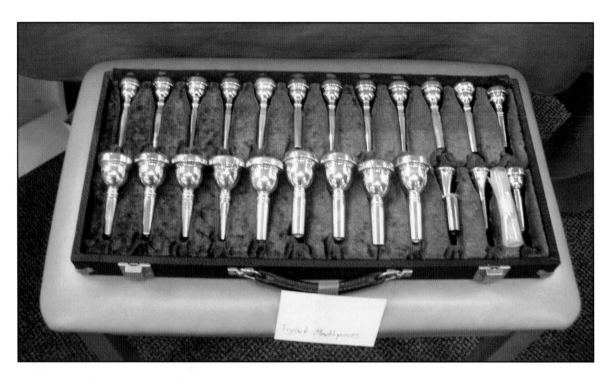

The leadpipe is the piece of tubing that goes from the mouthpiece to the valve slide. It is very important to keep the inside and the outside of the leadpipe clean. Any dent anywhere will affect the sound of the trumpet.

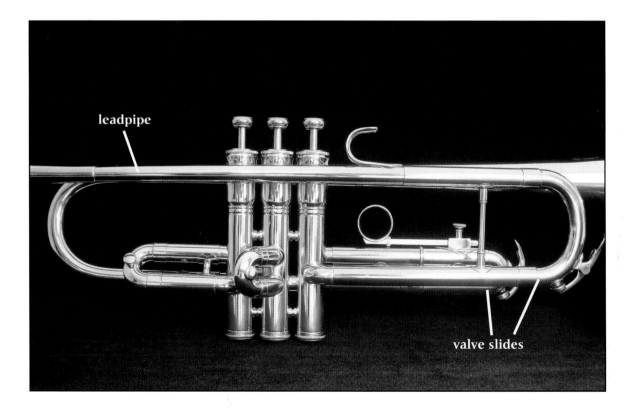

The sound of the trumpet is changed by routing air through the valve slides. This changes the length of the trumpet, and thus the sound of the note being played. To play the notes of the scale, the trumpet player must press the pistons. The one closest to the player is 1, the middle one is 2, and the one farthest away is 3. Each one is a little bit different in size. When cleaning and maintaining your trumpet, always be careful to replace each piston in the proper place.

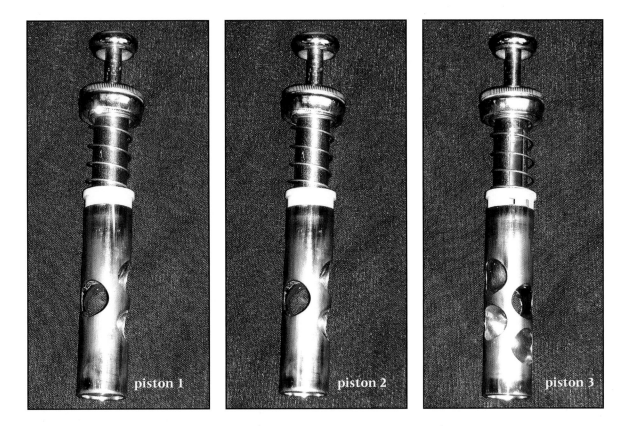

piston 1   piston 2   piston 3

The pistons need to be oiled regularly. You can purchase special valve oil for your trumpet at any music store.

The valve casings hold the pistons. It is important to keep the casings free of dents. If you should get a dent, take your trumpet to a qualified trumpet repairperson.

The finger hook, to the right of the valve casings, serves no musical purpose. It is simply a place to put the pinky of your right hand.

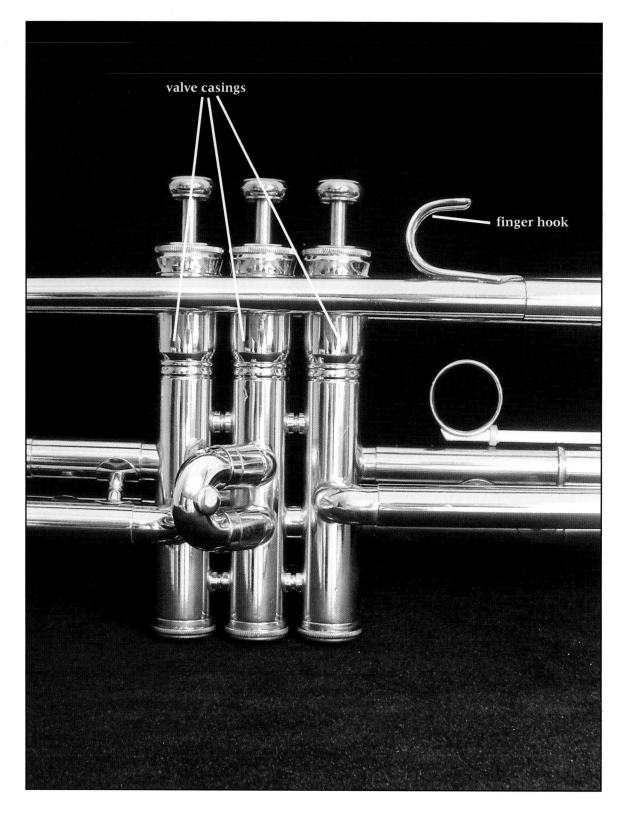

The tuning slide, or valve slide, can be adjusted to correct or fine tune the trumpet's sound.

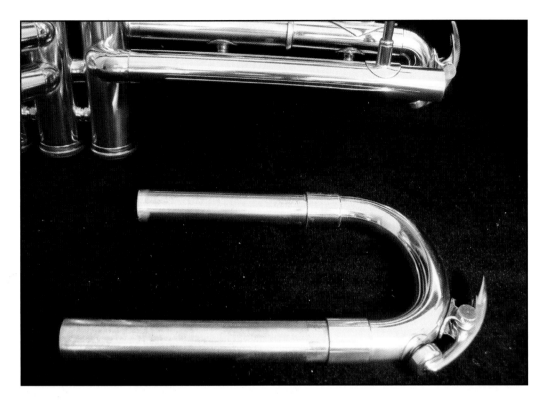

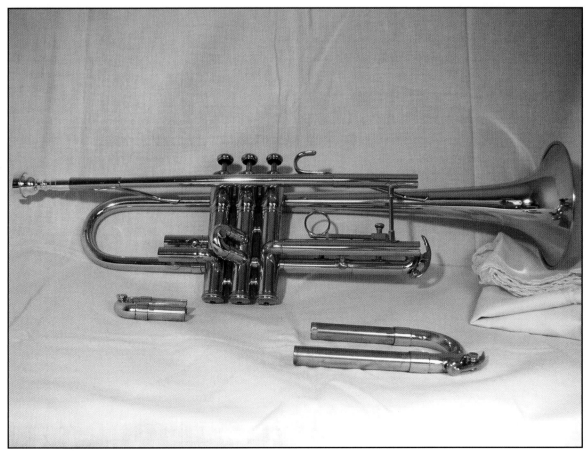

The spit valve is used to remove excess saliva from inside the trumpet. As the trumpet's tubing fills with spit, the instrument begins to gurgle. The spit valve must be opened regularly to clear out the moisture. Sometimes, a trumpet may have a spit valve on each slide.

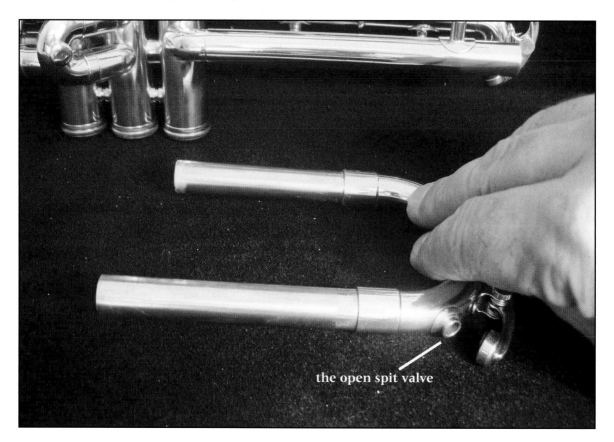

the open spit valve

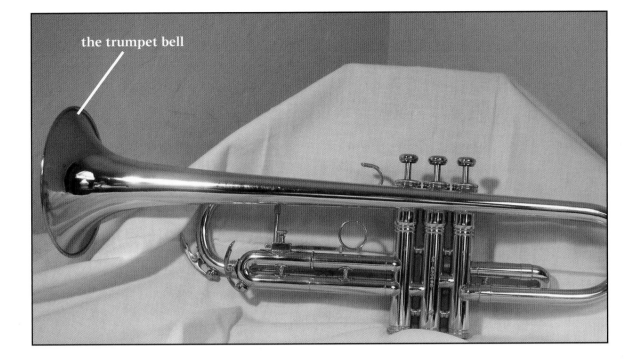

the trumpet bell

To clean the trumpet, the player must open the spit valve and breathe gently but steadily into the mouthpiece. This will force the moisture out of the valve. If you're playing with an orchestra or band, you can clean the spit valve when there is a pause in your part of the music, if necessary. Often, you will be able to wait until the musical piece is finished to clean out your trumpet. It is very important to clean the trumpet when you're finished practicing or playing, because over time it will damage the instrument.

The bell produces the sound of the trumpet. Most are made of brass, although some can be made of silver or bronze. The flare—the degree to which the bell gets wider and larger—affects the tone of the trumpet.

For information on how to care for your trumpet, see page 93.

PART TWO: GETTING READY to PLAY

1. Reading Music: The Basics

Everybody has to learn the following simple stuff about music. I'll make it as painless as possible, but you've got to put in some time.

The Staff

First of all, music is a language, and it is written on a staff. A staff has five lines and four spaces.

The lines and spaces each represent different notes, as shown below:

To give order to the music, the staff is divided into measures by vertical bar lines. Here is the staff with a G clef in 4/4 time and double bar line:

You know you're at the end of a section when you see a double bar line on the staff. In the illustration to the right, the two dots mean that the musician should go back and play the same section of music a second time.

Repeat Sign

One other thing you may see when you are reading music is a small number at the beginning of some measures (circled in red below). This is just a helpful guide for the musician; it lets you know what measure you are playing. This can be particularly useful when you are playing music with a group, and the leader or instructor wants to you to start at a particular measure, rather than at the beginning of the song. Although in this book the number appears above the staff at the first measure of each line of music, in other music you may find that the number appears at the bottom of the staff, or that each measure is numbered.

The Notes

Next we shall take a look at what gets written on the staff. The notes tell us what tones to play. A note has three parts.

The Head: gives a general indication of time: a hollow oval is a half note or a whole note, while a solid oval is a quarter note.

The Head

The Stem: all notes excluding whole notes have a stem.

The Stem

The Flag: the presence of a flag indicates an eighth or sixteenth note.

The Flag

You can find notes *on* the staff, *above* the staff, and *below* the staff. The note will take the name of the line or space it occupies on the staff. Where you put the note will indicate the pitch, which is the highness or lowness of the tone.

Quarter Note

A quarter note has a stem and a solid oval head. It usually gets one count. If there are four beats in the measure, you might count "one, two, three, four" in your mind when playing; the quarter note would generally be played for the amount of time it takes to count "one."

Notes with a stem and hollow oval head are called half notes. A half note gets two counts, or

Half Note   Eighth Note   Whole Note

beats, per measure. It is twice as long as a quarter note, so count "one, two."

An eighth note has a solid head, a stem, and a flag. Often, two eighth notes will be connected. The eighth note lasts half as long as a quarter note. So if you are mentally counting the beats in the measure, you would count "one and two and three and four and." Each of these words would represent an eighth note; you would play one eighth note on the "one" and a second on the "and."

A whole note is a hollow circle. It indicates a note that receives four beats.

Sometimes, you will see a dot next to a note, as shown in the lower left corner. This means that when you play the note, you need to add one-half the original value of the note to its length. For example, a dotted half note is

Dotted Half Note

played for three beats, while a dotted quarter note is extended by an extra eighth. (In 4/4 time each measure would have eight eighth notes; the dotted quarter note would be played for three eighths.)

Rests also appear in the measure. These symbols indicate to the musician when he or she should take a brief break from playing. Like notes, there are different symbols for rests, depending on how long the musician should be silent. Two common rests, quarter note and half note rests, are pictured below.

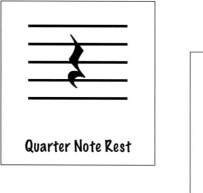

Quarter Note Rest

Half Note Rest

2. Finding the Notes

When you learn to read the notes in a piece of music, you will be able to communicate with musicians all around the world. First, though, you have to be able to recognize where each note appears on the staff.

The Lines

The note on the bottom line is E. The next line up is G, then B, then D, and F. To remember the order of these notes, many students memorize the phase: **E**very **G**ood **B**oy **D**eserves **F**udge.

The Spaces

The spaces from the bottom up are: F, A, C, E. Yes, it's the word "face."

Reading Them All Together

If you forget one or two, just remember that music uses only the letters A through G, and that the notes are always in alphabetical order. So if you start on the bottom line, E, the next space is F, the next line is G, and the following space is A. The next line will be B and so on.

Remember, notes can be written above and below the staff.

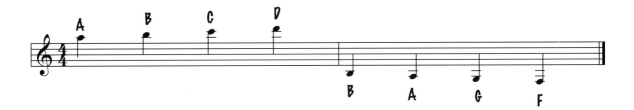

In the example above, some of the notes have an extra line or two through them, either above or below the five-line staff. These are called ledger lines, and they help the musician to easily identify the proper note.

3. Clef Symbols

Another thing that appears on the staff is called the clef. There are a couple of clefs. One is called the treble or G clef, which looks like this:

The Treble Clef

Another commonly used clef is the bass clef, but this is mostly found in piano and bass instrument music. However, it's still good to know the symbol in case you ever come across it. It looks like this:

The Bass Clef

The lines and spaces in bass clef have different lettering, but since we won't be using this for the trumpet, we can save that lesson for another time.

Let's Review

1. Music is written on a **staff**, which has **five** lines and **four** spaces.
2. The notes of the lines are **EGBDF.**
3. The notes of the spaces are **FACE.**
4. Trumpet music is normally written in the **treble clef.**
5. The staff is divided into **measures** by vertical lines called **bars.**

4. Time Signature

Anybody learning music has to know these basics, and we're almost done. Beyond the things we have already covered, you must also learn to read the time signature.

The time signature tells us how many beats there are in a measure and which beat gets "the one." That might not make any sense at all, but it will. Of all music you will see, 90 percent is either in 4/4 time or 3/4 time. So for now that's all you'll need to know.

The top number is the number of beats per measure. So in 4/4 time, there are four beats per measure. The bottom number tells us the type of note getting one beat (quarter note, half note, etc.). A four here means the quarter note gets one beat.

So if the top number was 6, it would mean there would be 6 beats per measure. And if the bottom number was 8, it would mean the eighth note counts as one beat.

| 2/4 Time | 4/4 Time (also known as common time) | 3/4 Time | 6/8 Time |

You will sometimes see a C in the place of a time signature. That simply stands for 4/4, or common time. Most of the music you will see is either in 4/4 or 3/4 time.

HELPFUL TIP:
Before you play, always look at the time signature to make sure you know the value of each note in a song.

5. The Sharp and Flat Signs

The figure on the F line in this picture is called a sharp. If you see it placed in front of a note, you should play the note a half step up. For example, if you see an F with the # before it, you would not play F, you would play the note a half tone higher. This note is called F#.

A flat sign looks like a small b. This means to play a note a half tone lower. Sharps and flats can indicate the same note. For instance, a Gb and an F# are the same tone.

If you see one sharp in the key signature (like in the top right), the music is in the key of G. If you see one flat in the key signature (as in the image above left), the music is in the key of F. Below are the sharps and flats that will appear in the key signatures of some other musical keys.

The Key of D   The Key of A   The Key of E   The Key of B

The Key of Bb   The Key of Eb   The Key of Ab   The Key of C

Sometimes a song may include a note or notes that are not in the same key as the rest of the song. When this happens, you will see a sharp or flat symbol next to the note in your music. If the note is already sharp or flat, you may see another symbol next to the note. This means to play the natural tone. Musicians call these notes "accidentals." As you see from the staff below, the symbols show the musician when to start and stop playing sharps and flats.

Natural Symbol

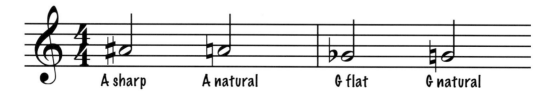

A sharp   A natural   G flat   G natural

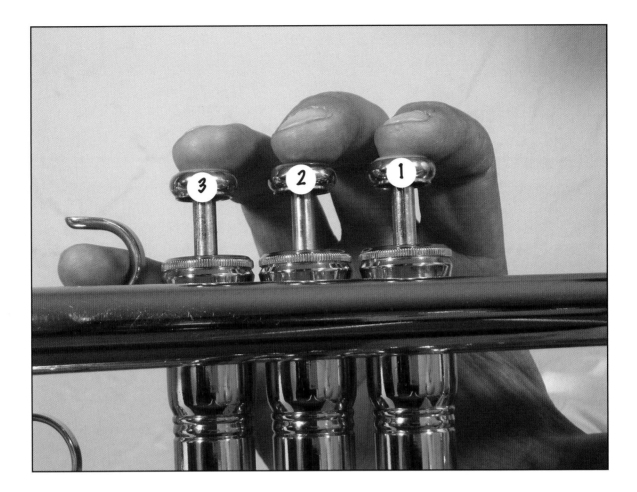

6. Holding the Trumpet

Your right hand is the hand that plays the trumpet and stabilizes the instrument. Place your index finger, or finger 1, over the valve closest to you. Place your middle finger, finger 2, over the middle valve, and your ring finger, finger 3, over the valve farthest away. Place your pinky in the finger hook. Your thumb will rest just below the first valve. Hold the trumpet with your pinky and your thumb. (See picture above)

Your left hand does most of the holding, as shown at right. Wrap your thumb around the first valve's casing about halfway down. Wrap your index, middle, and ring fingers around the casings as shown. (The ring finger could go in the finger ring.) Your pinky should fit under the trumpet tubing.

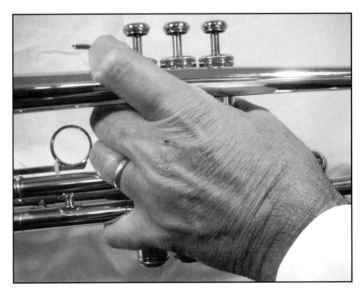

7. Blowing into the Trumpet

The most important part of playing any brass instrument is providing the air to make your instrument work. The last thing you should do is fill your lungs and cheeks with air and blow as hard as you can. Doing that a couple of times could hurt you. Here's how you should think of your breathing.

Imagine someone coming up to you and suddenly thrusting a finger at your belly button to poke you in the stomach. Your reaction would be to take a very quick but shallow breath in, because as the person's hand comes toward you, you suck in your belly quickly. The place that you instinctively sucked in is your diaphragm, just below your stomach. This is how I want you to control the air in and out of your body.

Don't keep any tension anywhere in your body, especially in your face. Most of your muscles should be relaxed. The only muscles that should be working are in your chest and around your lips.

You've felt how the air goes in and out according to the exercise above. Now slowly inhale and fill the area below your stomach and slowly let it out. Breathing is important to all musicians. Practice breathing slowly and deeply and letting the air out of your lungs slowly and smoothly.

HELPFUL HINT:
Pretend you have a small piece of popcorn on the end of your tongue that you want to spit off. As you breathe out, try to keep it going as long as possible. Bring your lips closer together, keep your tongue behind your teeth, and make a buzz sound.

8. Playing the Trumpet

The next step is to practice your breathing with the mouthpiece only. This gets you used to breathing and gives your lips a chance to practice buzzing. Practicing this way also helps build the muscles around your mouth, which you will need to play the trumpet. Lip buzzing, a technique detailed on p. 90, should be part of your daily practice drills.

Next, gently place the mouthpiece in the trumpet. Do not pop it in with the palm of your hand. Gently place it in the trumpet and gently turn it in. If you jam the mouthpiece in and it becomes stuck, take it to an instrument repairperson. Do not pull or jerk the mouthpiece, as this could damage the mouthpiece or trumpet.

Once you feel comfortable holding the trumpet and have done a little breathing, gently bring the trumpet up to your lips.

Place the mouthpiece lightly against your lips. Once the mouthpiece is in place and feels comfortable it should not have to be moved. You should not have to move the trumpet around to get different notes. You may find you have to press the trumpet a wee bit harder on the lips to get a little more tension to help produce higher tones. But once you find the right place on your lips, it's not a good idea to move the trumpet around.

Now take a breath and blow firmly, but not hard, into the trumpet. You need to make a buzzing with your lips in order to make a sound. Try for a while until you are able to start making a nice, full tone. By doing this you should get the sound of either the note C or G. The higher sounding note will be the G, the lower note is Middle C. The pictures below show what the notes look like on the staff:

Middle C (half note) and rest

G (half note) and rest

Remember, both notes are played open—don't press any valves down.

You may ask, "How can I make two different sounds without using the valves?" The trick is increasing the flow of air from your lungs. Blowing a little harder and closing your lips slightly will allow you to do this.

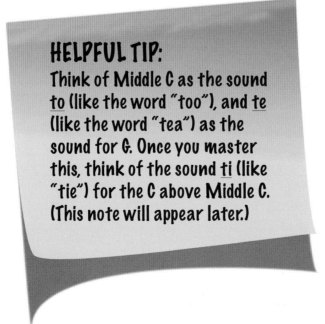

HELPFUL TIP:
Think of Middle C as the sound to (like the word "too"), and te (like the word "tea") as the sound for G. Once you master this, think of the sound ti (like "tie") for the C above Middle C. (This note will appear later.)

9. First Practice Pieces

Here are your first practice pieces. You need to practice playing the notes C and G until you can play them clearly and cleanly. Remember, in 4/4 time whole notes receive all four beats in each measure. Half notes are played for two beats, quarter notes get one beat, and eighth notes get a half-beat. (In other words, you can play two eighth notes in the same time it takes to play a quarter note.)

C, half notes

C, quarter notes, exercise 1

Things to Remember

1. Take a nice deep breath from your diaphragm
2. Close your mouth lightly
3. Keep your lips together

C, eighth notes and whole notes

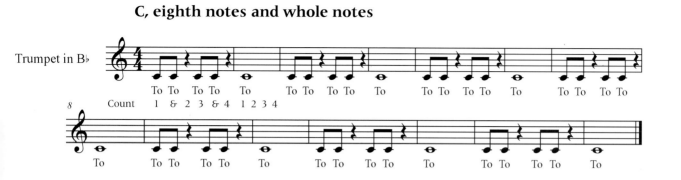

C, dotted half notes (remember, with a half note the dot adds one beat; play on beats one, two, and three, and rest on four.)

C, quarter and whole notes, exercise 2

G, half notes

G, quarter notes, exercise 1

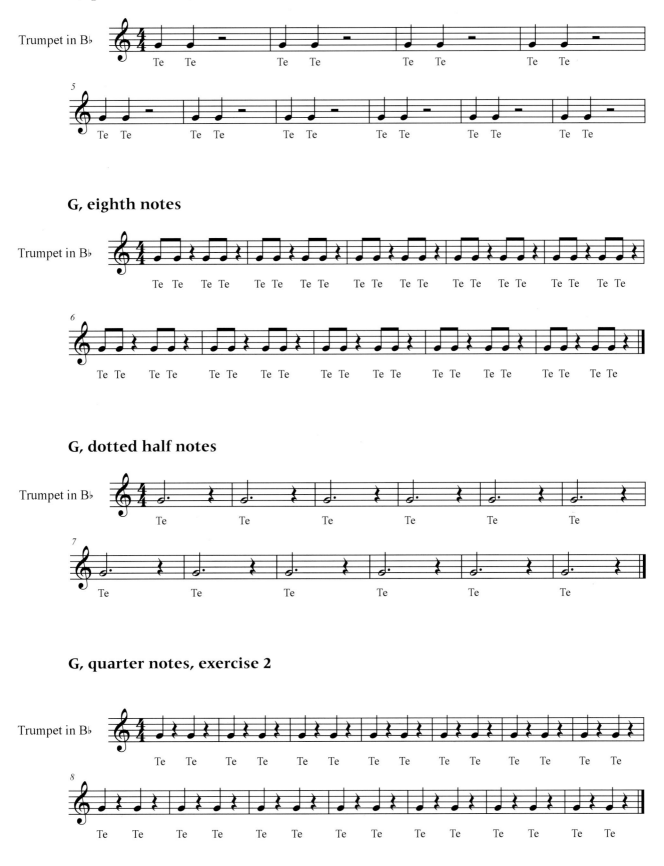

G, eighth notes

G, dotted half notes

G, quarter notes, exercise 2

C and G, half notes, exercise 1

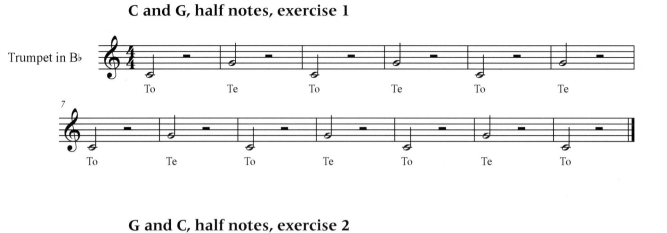

G and C, half notes, exercise 2

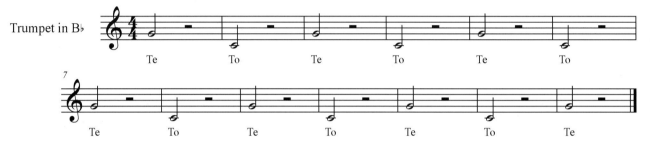

C and G, quarter notes, exercise 1

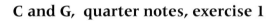
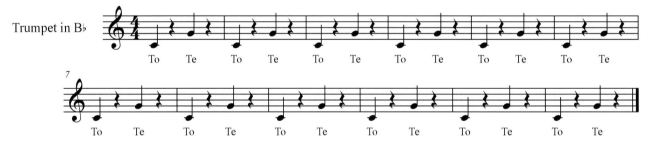

G and C, quarter notes, exercise 2

C and G, eighth notes and whole notes, exercise 1

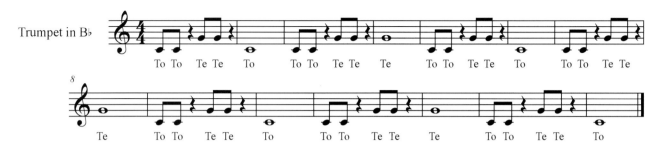

G and C, eighth notes and whole notes, exercise 2

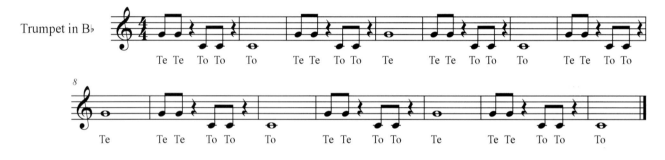

C and G, "Mixing it Up"

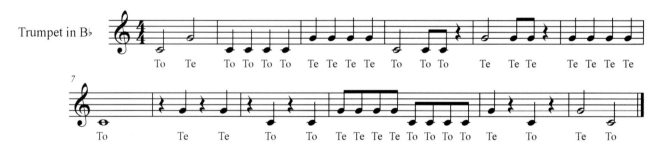

C and G, "The Trumpet Call"

PART THREE:

LET'S PLAY!

1. The Note D

Now that you can play a C and a G we can move on to notes that require using the valves. Play the C. As you blow, blow a bit harder or stronger with your first and third fin-

D (half note) and rest

gers pressing down. You should now be playing the note D.

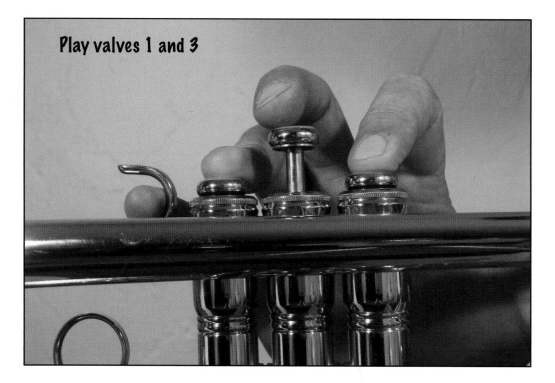

Play valves 1 and 3

2. D Exercises

Practice playing the D just like the C and G until you can play it cleanly and clearly. Here are some exercises for D.

D, half notes

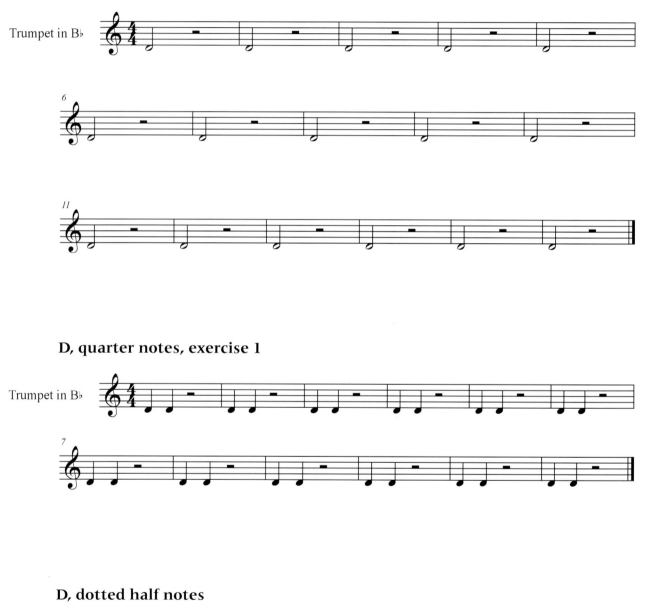

D, quarter notes, exercise 1

D, dotted half notes

D, quarter notes, exercise 2

D, eighth notes and whole notes

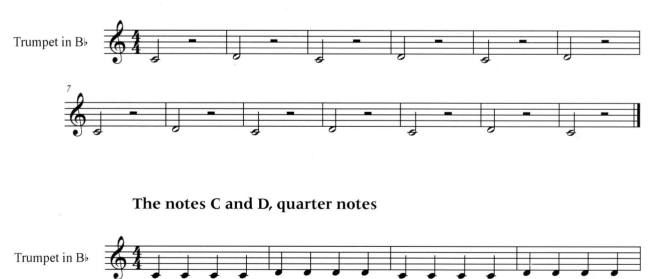

The notes C and D, half notes Here you play the C, which is open (no valves), and then the D.

The notes C and D, quarter notes

The notes C, D, and G, half notes, exercise 1

The notes C, D, and G, half notes, exercise 2

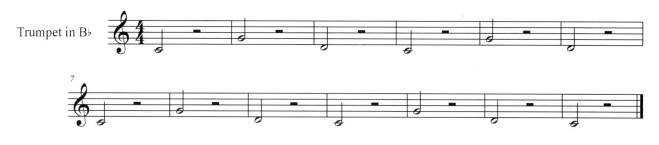

The notes C, D, and G, quarter notes

KEEP IN MIND:
As you begin to practice these exercises, start slowly and play each note clearly.

3. The Note F

Now play the note G again, but this time, blow a bit harder and press the first valve down. You should be playing the note F.

F (half note) and rest

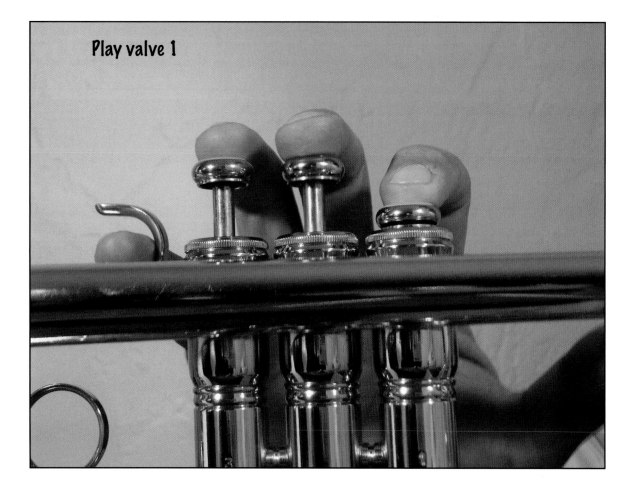

Play valve 1

4. F Exercises

Here are some exercises you can use to help you practice playing F:

F, half notes

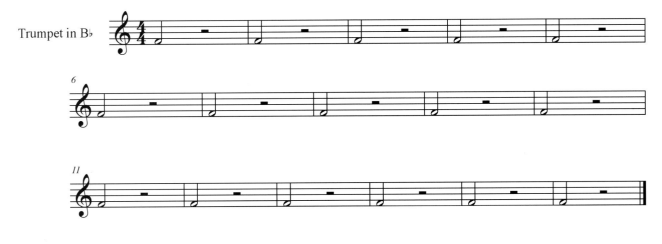

F, quarter notes

F, eighth notes

5. The Note E

As you play a G or a C, find a place between the two and press the first and second valves. This note will be more of a feeling than anything else. You know what it feels like to play a G, and you know what it feels like to play a C. Now you are looking for some place in between these two notes. When you find it, you should get the note E.

E (half note) and rest

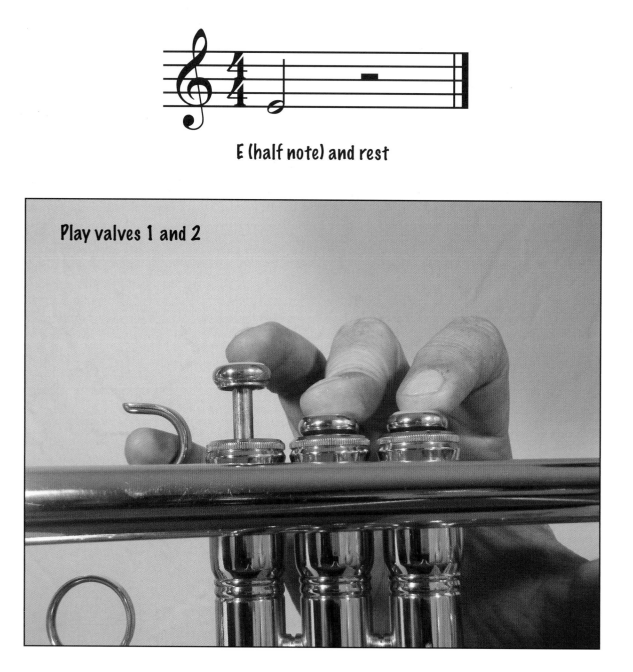

Play valves 1 and 2

6. E Exercises

The first exercises on the next few pages will help you practice playing the note E by itself. Then you'll have to practice playing the note along with others that you've learned.

E, half notes

E, quarter notes, exercise 1

E, quarter notes, exercise 2

The notes C, D, and E, quarter notes

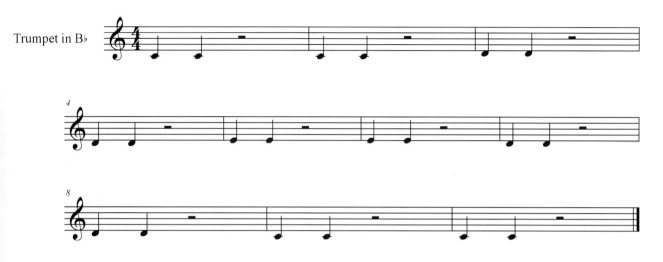

C, D, E, and F, quarter notes

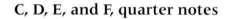

C, D, E, F, and G, quarter notes, exercise 1

C, D, E, F, and G, quarter notes, exercise 2

C, D, E, F, and G, half notes, exercise 1

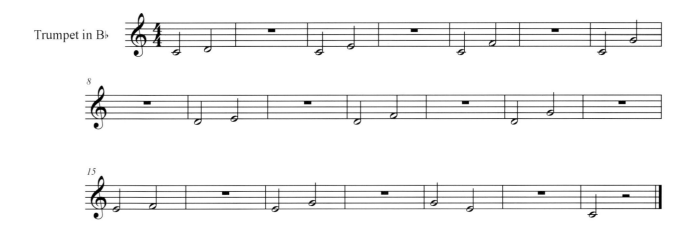

C, D ,E, F, and G, half notes, exercise 2

C, D, E, F, and G, dotted quarters and eighth notes Remember, the dot adds one-half the value of the note. This adds an extra eighth to the quarter note, giving it a value of one-and-a-half-beats.

When the Saints Go Marching In

Trumpet in B♭

Oh when the Saints go march ing in, oh when the Saints go march ing in. Lord I

want to be in that numb er, when the Saints go march ing in.

DID YOU KNOW?

The first version of the song "When the Saints Go Marching In" was published in 1896. The music was written by James Milton Black, while the original lyrics were credited to Katharine Purvis. However, there have been many different variations of the lyrics.

Although "When the Saints Go Marching In" is a Christian hymn that often appears in church songbooks, it has also been a Dixieland jazz standard for nearly a century. The song is closely identified with the city of New Orleans, where the Dixieland style of jazz developed in the early 20th century. A distinctive feature of the Dixieland sound is that one instrument (usually the trumpet) plays the melody of the song (or a slight variation), while the other musicians (usually playing guitar or banjo, string bass or tuba, piano, and drums) improvise around that melody.

During the 1930s, the famous trumpeter Louis Armstrong (pictured) hit the pop charts with his recording of the song. Many other singers have recorded or performed the song as well, including Judy Garland, Fats Domino, Jerry Lee Lewis, The Beatles, Elvis Presley, and Bruce Springsteen.

C, D, E, F, and G, quarter notes, exercise 3

C, D, E, F, and G, quarter notes, exercise 4

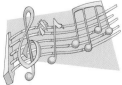

C, D, E, F, and G, half notes, exercise 3

C, D, E, F, and G, half notes, exercise 4

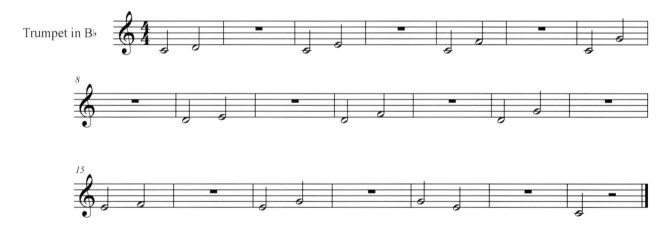

Hint for Reading Music

Many songs (including "When the Saints Go Marching In" on page 47) begin with what are called pick-up notes. When that happens, the song doesn't begin at the start of the first measure. In "When the Saints" there are three half notes in the first measure, so you would count "one-and-two-and-three" before playing on the "and-four-and" beats.

7. The Bb Trumpet

If you were to go to a piano and play the notes Bb, C, D, Eb, and F, they will sound like the notes you have been playing C, D, E, F, and G. Your trumpet is called a B-flat trumpet because it is tuned to the key of Bb, meaning the first note in the harmonic series of the trumpet is actually Bb. However, when you see written music for a trumpet, this note is written as a C.

Sometimes this can be a problem. A beginning trumpet player must be careful when reading music written for the piano, for stringed instruments, or for vocalists. To play this music properly, the trumpet player must transpose it into the correct key. This is done by playing every note one step higher than the note that appears in the music.

Don't worry about this if you are just starting. All of the music in this book, as well as practically all sheet music written specifically for trumpet players, has already been transposed to the proper key.

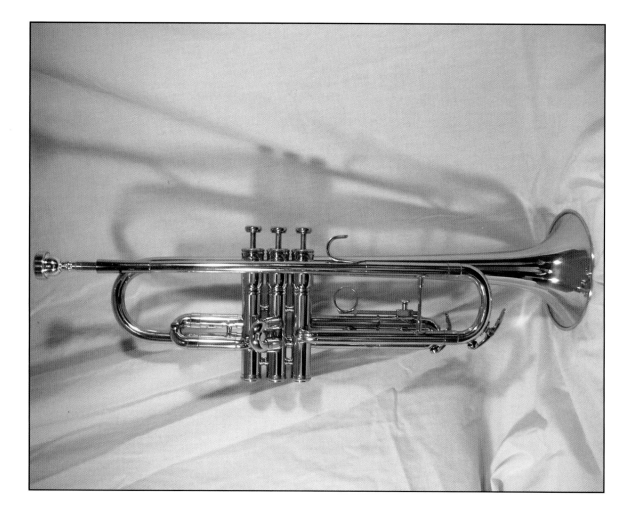

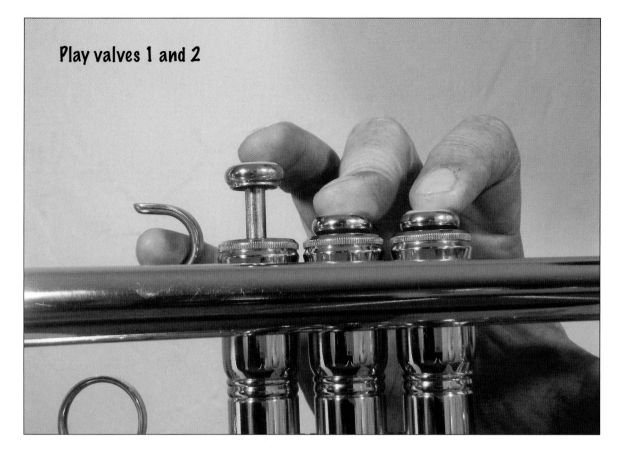

Play valves 1 and 2

8. The Note A

Play a G on the trumpet and blow a bit harder while pressing the first and second valves. You should get the note A. Again, practice the note until you play it clearly and cleanly.

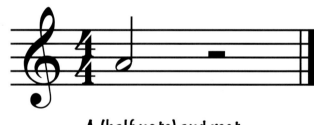

A (half note) and rest

9. A Exercises

Following are some exercises that will help you to play the note A, along with some songs that use A and the other notes you've learned so far:

A, half notes

Trumpet in B♭

A, quarter notes

A, eighth notes

Trumpet in B♭

The notes G and A, half notes

Trumpet in B♭

Watch the sixteenth
notes in the fifth
and sixth measures.

This Old Man

Traditional English

This old man   he played one,   he   played knick knack   on   my thumb

Knick   knack   pad dy whack,   Give a dog a bone,   this old man came   roll ing home.

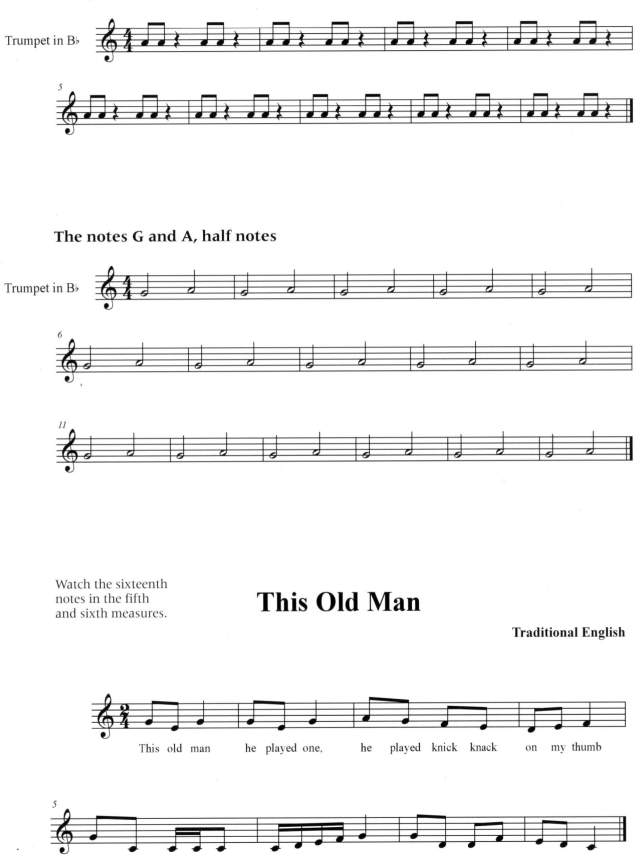

Aupres de ma Blonde

France

HELPFUL TIP:
Remember, you will know that your music has already been transposed if at the very top left hand corner or next to the staff it says "Bb trumpet."

C, D, E, F, G, and A, half notes, exercise 1

C, D, E, F, G, and A, half notes, exercise 2

C, D, E, F, G, and A, quarter notes, exercise 1

C, D, E, F, G, and A, quarter notes, exercise 2

10. The Note B

Play the note A again, and with a little more air, release the first valve. Keep the second valve pressed and you should be playing the note B.

B (half note) and rest

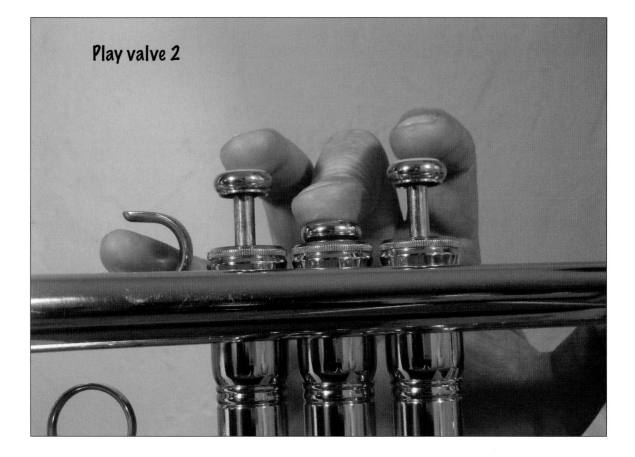

Play valve 2

11. B Exercises

Following are some exercises that will help you to play the note B.

B, half notes

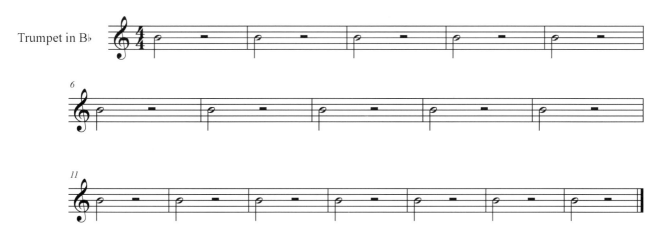

B, quarter notes

B, eighth notes

12. The Note F#

Remember on page 26 when we discussed the different keys in which music can be written? If you want to play a song that's written in the key of G (pictured at right), you'll have to be able to play the note F#.

The Key of G

Start by playing the note F, first valve down. Now lift your first finger and with your middle finger press the second valve down. This is F#.

F# (half note) and rest

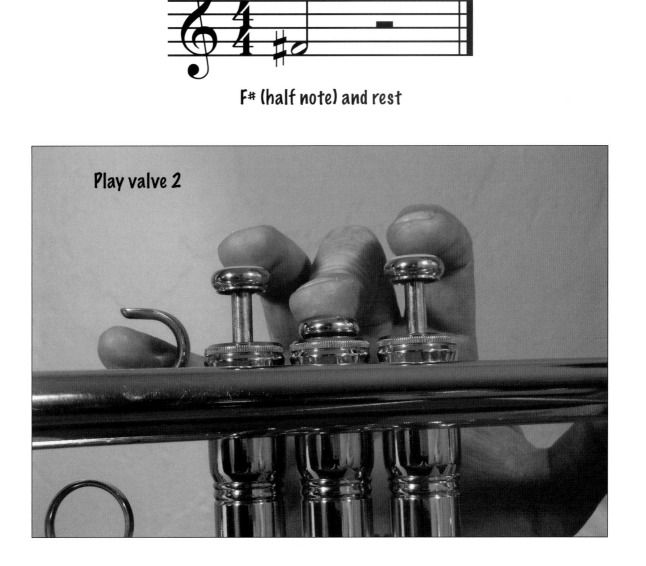

Play valve 2

If you do want to play in the key of G, remember that all of the Fs are sharp unless you see a natural sign in front of the note.

13. F# Exercises

F#, half notes

F#, quarter notes

F#, eighth notes

G and F#, half notes

G and F#, quarter notes

C, D, E, F#, and G, half notes

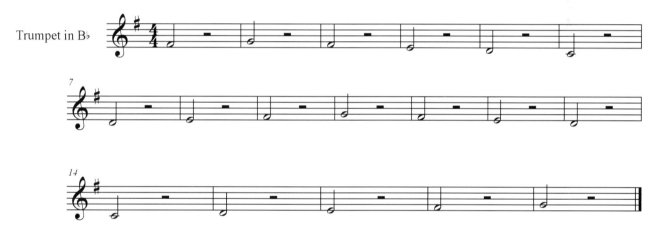

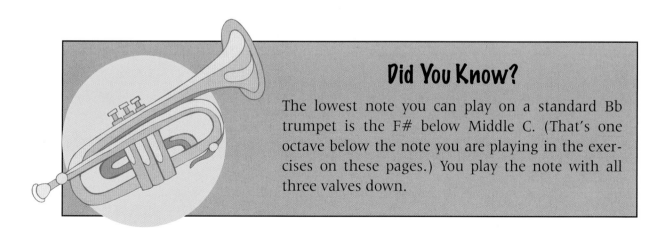

Did You Know?

The lowest note you can play on a standard Bb trumpet is the F# below Middle C. (That's one octave below the note you are playing in the exercises on these pages.) You play the note with all three valves down.

14. The Note C above Middle C

Now that you can play the notes C, D, E, F, G, A, and B, you're ready to try playing notes that have a higher pitch. Trumpeters refer to this as playing in a higher register.

The C above Middle C is played by applying a bit more air pressure and getting the lips a bit closer as you play G. Doing this should enable you to hit the C above Middle C.

C above Middle C (half note) and rest

15. C above Middle C Exercises

Following are some exercises that will help you to play the C above Middle C. Once you've mastered that note, you'll be able to play many more songs.

C above Middle C, half notes

Helpful Tip

If you recall, when you learned your first two notes, C and G, you were instructed to think of the sound *to* (like the word "too") for Middle C and the sound *te* (like the word "tea") for G. Now, you can think of the sound *ti* (like "tie") for the C above Middle C.

C above Middle C, quarter notes

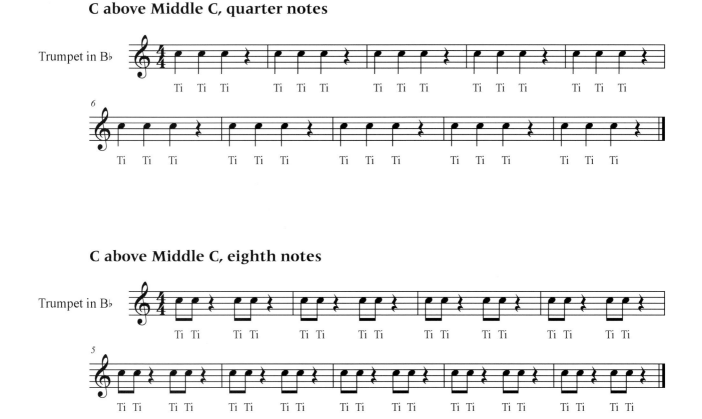

Once you're comfortable playing the C above Middle C, use the following exercises to practice switching from Middle C to the C above Middle C. (Musicians call this playing octaves.)

Middle C to C above Middle C, half notes

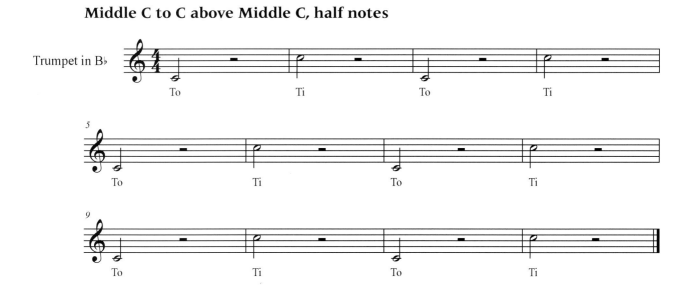

C, G, and C above Middle C, half notes, exercise 1

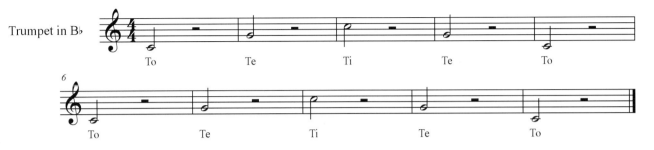

C, G, and C above Middle C, half notes, exercise 2

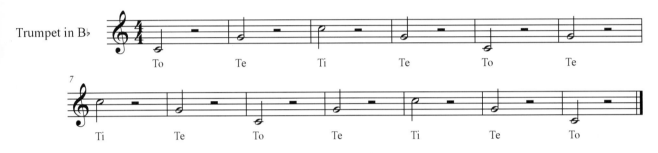

C, G, and C above Middle C, quarter notes, exercise 1

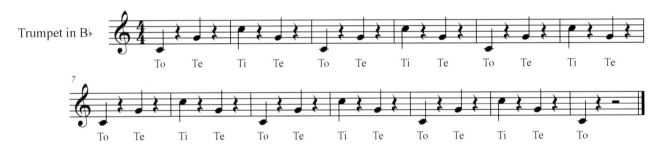

Note Fingerings

The following are the fingerings for the notes from Middle C to the C above Middle C:

C (Middle C): 0	G: 0
D: 1-3	A: 1-2
E: 1-2	B: 2
F: 1	C above Middle C: 0

C, G, and C above Middle C, quarter notes, exercise 2

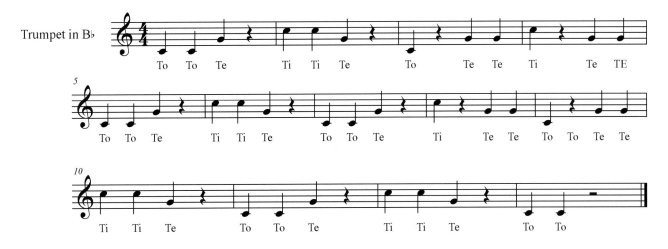

Now you're ready to play the following songs, many of which you probably already know.

Jacob's Ladder

Spiritual

Camptown Races

Stephen Foster

Trumpet in B♭

The Camp town la dies sing this song, do dah, do dah. The

Camp town race track five miles long, oh, do dah, day.

Goin' to run all night. Goin' to run all day. I

bet my mon ey on the bob tail nag, some bo dy bet on the bay.

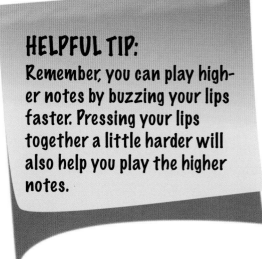

HELPFUL TIP:
Remember, you can play higher notes by buzzing your lips faster. Pressing your lips together a little harder will also help you play the higher notes.

Sakura

Japan

Tipalo Bend

American folk

The Bugle Call

The bugle is a brass instrument related to the trumpet. Unlike the trumpet, the bugle does not have valves to enable the player to control the pitch of notes. Instead, the bugler plays different notes by using the facial muscles in different ways. Bugles have been used in the military for centuries. The picture at left shows an American cavalryman rallying his comrades with a bugle call (circa 1860–1875); the opposite page is an Army recruiting poster from the First World War.

Men Wanted
for the Army

APPLY AT

Recruiting St   ion.

Trumpet Salute

Trumpet Salute 2

HELPFUL TIP:
It takes practice to be able to play any of the higher notes. You need to exercise the muscles around your lips so they have the strength to buzz faster. This will take some time. Playing too much or blowing too hard could hurt your lips, so practice a little at a time to get your embouchure in shape. (See page 92 for ways to develop these muscles.)

Old MacDonald Had a Farm

American

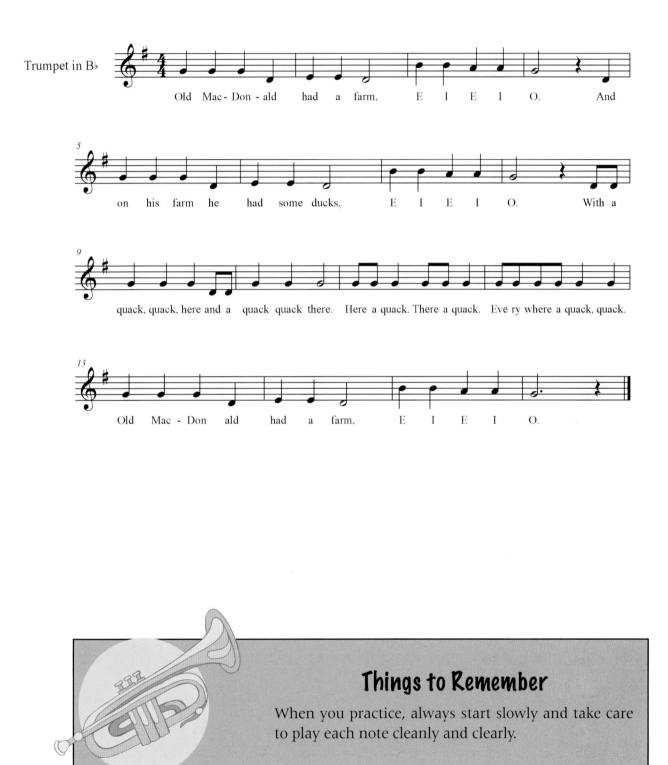

Things to Remember

When you practice, always start slowly and take care to play each note cleanly and clearly.

16. The C Major Scale

Now that you can play the C above Middle C, you should learn the C major scale. This could also be called the concert Bb major scale.

Starting on the Low C and ending on the C above Middle C, the scale goes up in whole steps and half steps. (A whole step up from C is D, a half step up from C is C# or Db.) Any major scale's order is whole step, whole step, half step, whole step, whole step, whole step, half step.

Because of the way the trumpet is tuned, the C scale has no sharps or flats. It is C, D, E, F, G, A, B, C.

The C Scale, half notes

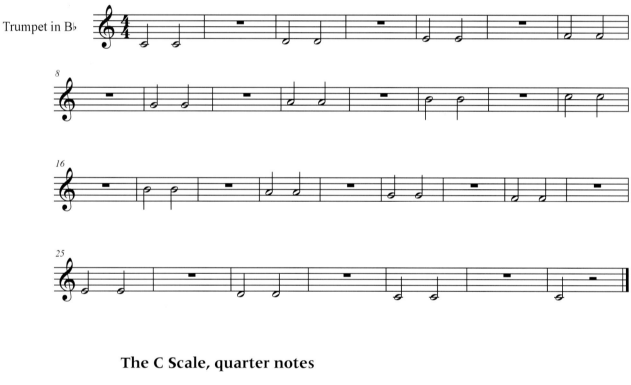

The C Scale, quarter notes

17. The Note Upper D

The next several notes you will learn are described as "upper" notes. This is meant as a way to easily differentiate them from the middle range notes you have already learned. They are not the highest notes you can play, but they will be challenging for beginners.

You already know how to play the D pictured in the staff at top right, with the first and third valves down.

To play the Upper D, which is shown on the lower staff, you need to provide more air via the

D (half note) and rest

Upper D (half note) and rest

pressure through your lips and change the fingering. The Upper D is played with just the first valve down, as the illustration below shows.

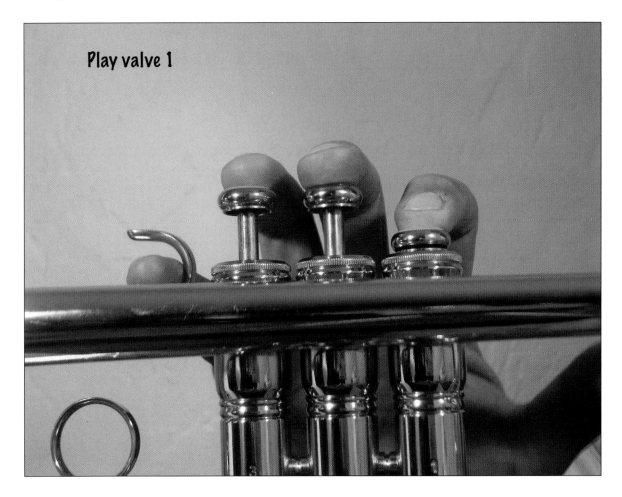

Play valve 1

18. Upper D Exercises

Following are some exercises that will help you to play the Upper D, as well as some more songs to practice. Once you've mastered that note, you'll be able to play many more songs. Several popular tunes are included at the end of this section.

Upper D, half notes

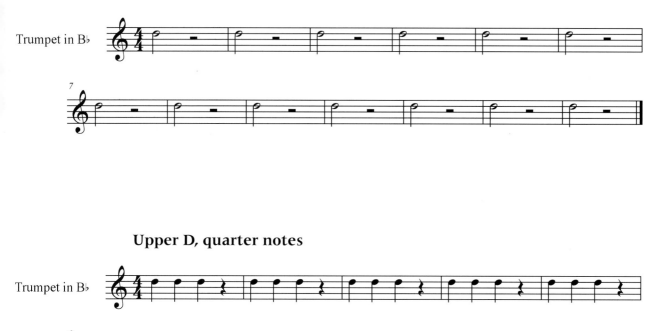

Upper D, quarter notes

Upper D, eighth notes

D to Upper D, half notes

D to Upper D, quarter notes

Clementine

Stephen Foster

I do love you, oh my dar ling, oh my dar ling so di

vine. You are lost and gone for ev er, oh my dar ling, Clem en tine.

19. The Note Upper E

The Upper E is played open. To start, play the low E, pressing the first and second valves. Now, with more air pressure, release the valves and close your lips a bit. This is the Upper E.

Upper E (half note) and rest

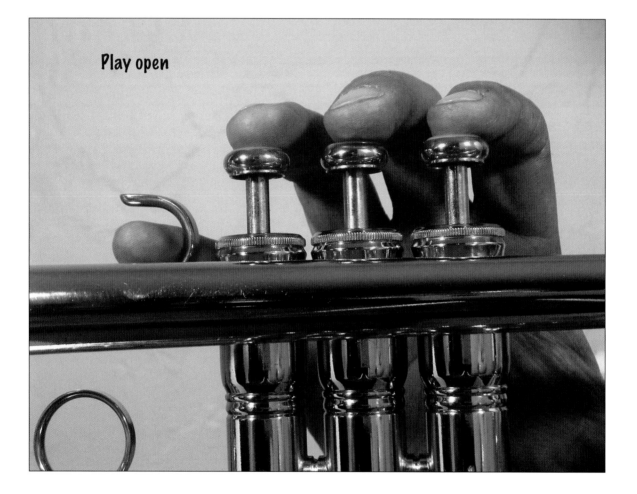

Play open

20. Upper E Exercises

Following are some exercises that will help you to play the Upper E, as well as some more songs to practice. Once you've mastered that note, you'll be able to play many more songs. Several popular tunes are included at the end of this section.

Upper E, half notes

Upper E, quarter notes

Upper E, eighth notes

E to Upper E, half notes

E to Upper E, quarter notes

Banyan Tree

Jamaica

Moon shine to night come mek we dance an sing. Moon shine to

night come mek we dance and sing. Me do rock so you do rock so un der ban yan tree

Me do rock so you do rock so un der ban yan tree.

Loch Lomond, Ye Take the High Road

Scotland

Trumpet in B♭

By yon bon nie bon ie banks and yon bon nie bon nie braes, where the

sun shine s bright on Loch Lo mond, whe re me and my true love will

ev er wont to gaze, on the bonnie bon nie banks of Loch Lo mond. Oh ye take the high road, and

I'll take the low. And I'll be in Scot land a fore ye. For me and my true love will

nev er meet a gain on the bon nie bon nie banks of Loch Lo mond.

All Through the Night

Old Welsh Tune

Sleep my child and peace a tend thee, all through the night. Guard ian an gels

God will send thee, all through the night. Soft ly so the hours are creep ing,

hill and dale in slum ber steep ing. I, my lov ing vi gil keep ing, all through the night.

Little Boy

Old English

Lit tle boy, lit tle boy come and find a place for your coat.

Lit tle boy you are ve ry sweet. Find a place for your hat and coat. Lit tle boy you

are ve ry young. Lit tle boy, Lit tle boy, come and find a place for your coat.

21. The Note Upper F

This note is played with the first valve down only.

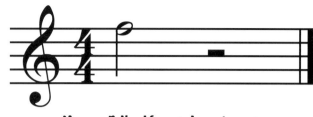

Upper F (half note) and rest

Play valve 1

22. Upper F Exercises

Upper F, half notes

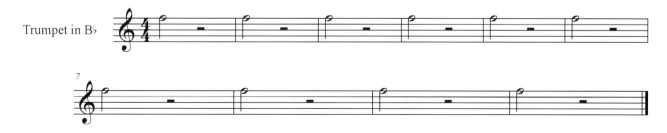

Upper F, quarter notes

Upper F, eighth notes

Upper F, half, quarter, and eighth notes

Did You Know?

In 1796 Joseph Haydn composed one of the first pieces of orchestra music to feature the trumpet, "Trumpet Concerto in E Flat Major."

23. The Note Upper F#

This note is played with the second valve down.

Upper F# (half note) and rest

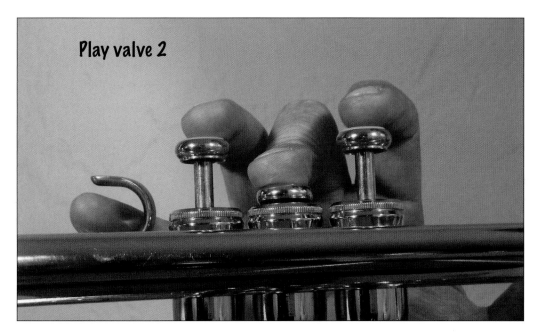

Play valve 2

24. Upper F# Exercises

F# to Upper F#, half notes

Upper D, E, F#, and G, half notes

25. The Note Upper G

You may already have discovered how to play the Upper G by accident when playing the G in the middle register (see page 30). Like G, the Upper G note is played with all valves open. Hitting the Upper G

Upper G (half note) and rest

requires more air pressure than G, so you'll need to use a little more air to produce the higher note. Also, make the space between your lips slightly smaller than when you play G in the middle register.

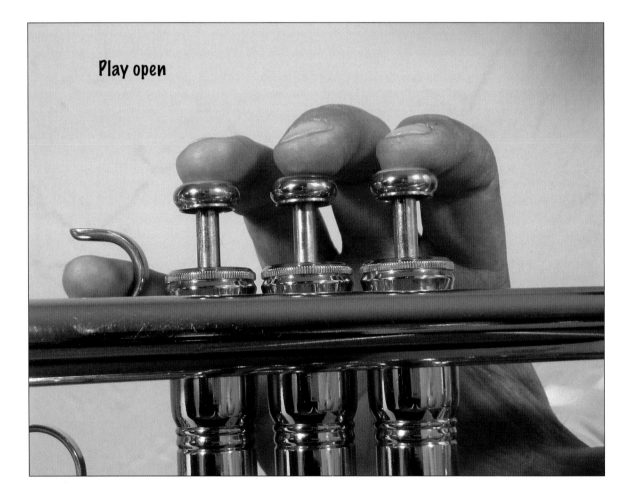

Play open

26. Upper G Exercises

Upper G, half notes

Upper G, quarter notes

Upper G, eighth notes

G to Upper G, half notes

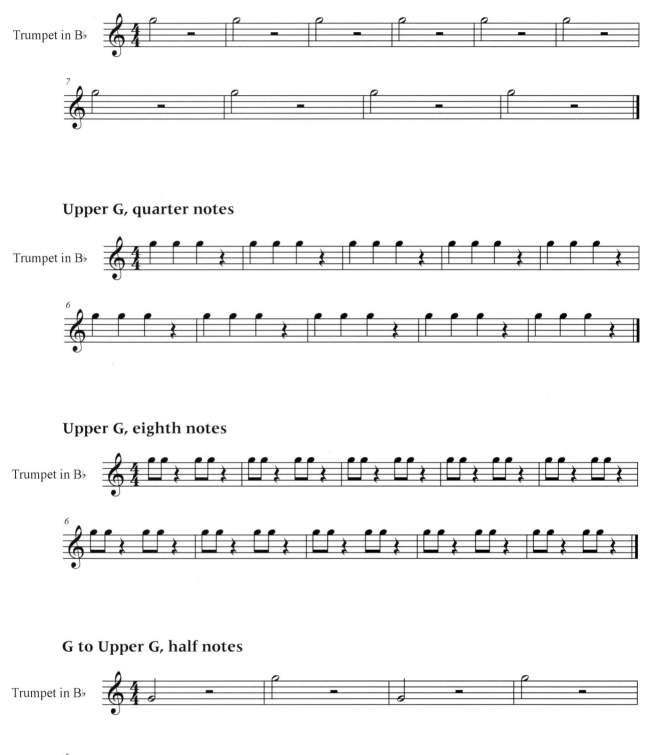

27. The Key of G

You will need to practice playing the notes D, E, F# and G to play songs written in the key of G. The key of a song will tell you if certain notes are sharp or flat throughout, rather than having to specify at each note. In the key of G, F notes are sharp, which will be marked at the beginning. Every time you see an F on the staff, you will play an F#.

The G Scale, quarter notes starting on C

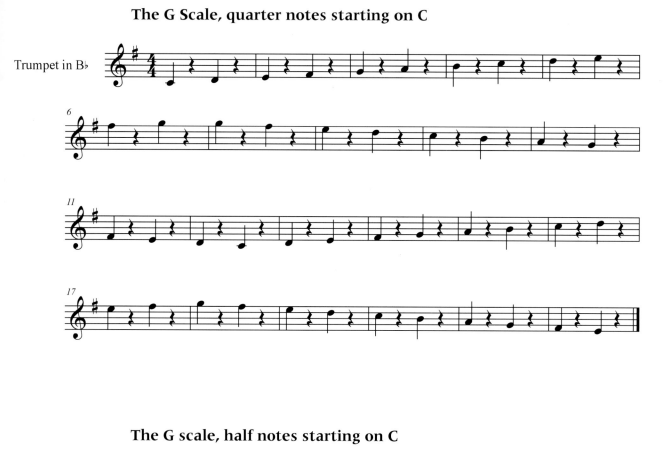

The G scale, half notes starting on C

28. The Notes Upper A and Upper B

To play the Upper A or the Upper B, use the same fingering as the A or B notes, but apply more pressure from the diaphragm and a little less space between the lips.

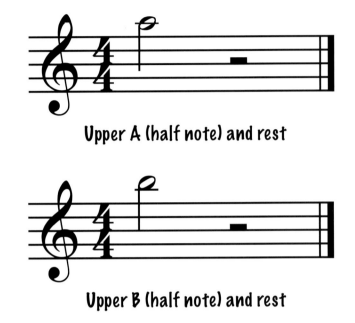

Upper A (half note) and rest

Upper B (half note) and rest

29. Upper A and Upper B Exercises

Following are some exercises that you can use to practice.

Upper A, half notes

Upper B, half notes

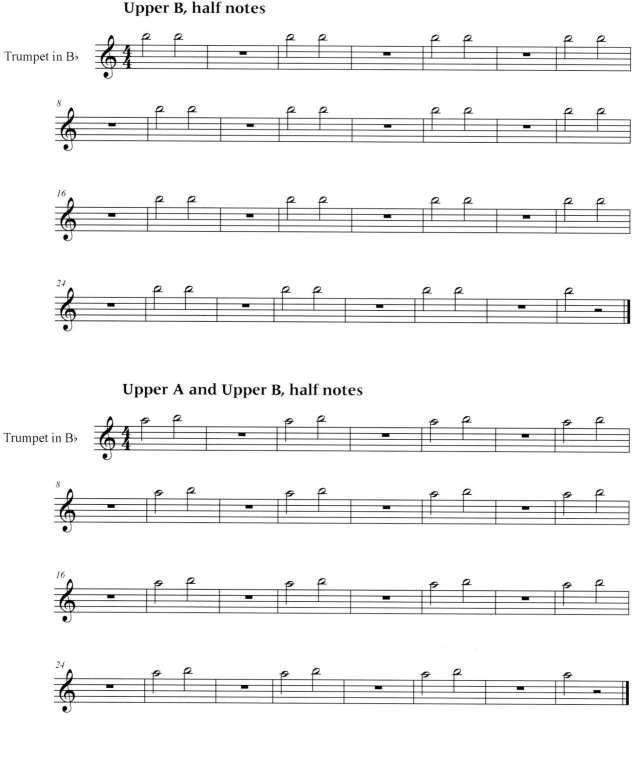

Upper A and Upper B, half notes

Upper G and A, half notes

Upper D, E, F#, and G, quarter notes

30. Embouchure Hints:

The proper use of the muscles around your face needed to play the trumpet is called your embouchure. (Musicians sometimes call this your "chops.") Here are some tips to help you strengthen and develop your facial muscles. They will help make you a better trumpet player:

1. Lip buzzing: This helps build the embouchure. Hold your lips as if you were playing the trumpet and get the air flowing and keep it constant. This also helps tune your ear to make a tone without the use of the valves.
2. Flap your lips: Pretend you're a horse. Sigh with your lips really relaxed and let them flap.
3. Practicing with just the mouthpiece: This gets your lips and mouth in shape and should show you that you don't need a lot of pressure to play.
4. Lip slurs: Once you have the mouthpiece in the trumpet, play the open C and G and try to play notes in between without using the valves. This really works your embouchure.
5. Tongue exercises: Stop and start the tone by using the tip of your tongue to stop or allow the flow of air.
6. Playing softly: This really helps strengthen the upper lip. It requires a lot of discipline to keep the tone going while playing softly.

Here are some things to keep in mind as you work on your embouchure:

1. Keep the corners of your month as relaxed as possible. Do not stretch them or expand them in any way.
2. Find a good place for the mouthpiece to rest against your lips. Try different places on your lips or a different angle. Find one that feels comfortable and produces the best sound.
3. Lightly touch your tongue to the back of your lips.

There are also some things that you should avoid. When practicing, DO NOT:

1. Fill your cheeks, chest, shoulders, and stomach up with air and blow. If you watch most trumpet players they don't do anything like that. Having said that, a few, like Dizzy Gillespie and Harry James, did perfect a style where they would fill their cheeks with air, but most do not.
2. Press your mouthpiece too hard against your lips.
3. Slouch. Always stand up straight or sit up straight. Imagine

the passageway of air from your lungs to the bell as a single tube. By standing crooked or sitting crooked, you're twisting the passageway and altering the flow of air.

4. Tense up. Relax all your muscles, especially in the throat and face.

5. Let your tongue go past your teeth.

31. Cleaning and Caring for Your Trumpet

1. Drain all the fluid from the trumpet. This is done by pressing the spit valve and gently blowing into the mouthpiece.

2. Take out the valves by unscrewing the tops of the valve covers and lifting each valve out gently. Make sure the valves are in working order by pressing down the key; it should spring right back. Spray a little valve oil on the valves so that they don't stick. Be careful as you put the valves back in, because they are not the same size. If the valves seem to be in proper working order when they are out of the trumpet, but stick when replaced, there may be a dent in the valve casing. In that case, you will have to take your instrument to a person experienced in trumpet repair.

3. When you take the trumpet apart, rub a little bit of slide grease, which can be purchased at any music store, on the slide tubing parts before you put them back together.

4. You should use a fine wire brush to carefully clean the mouthpiece.

5. If you want to shine the trumpet, use a silver cleaning cloth. (Selmer trumpet company also makes a cloth for this.) Do not use polish. You don't have to do this very often; perhaps once a year.

HELPFUL TIP:
Remember, regular cleaning and maintenance of your trumpet will ensure that it works properly and lasts longer.

PART FOUR

SONGS and EXERCISES

The following section contains a number of well-known songs which you can practice—and maybe even play for your friends or family some day. Remember, all great trumpet players started as beginners. Enjoy making music!

Golden Slumbers

Traditional English

Cielito Lindo

Mexico

Trumpet in B♭

From si er____ ra Mo re na, Cie____ li to Lin do, comes____ solf ly

steal ing._____ Laugh ing eyes____ black and ro guish, Cie____ li to

Lin do, beau____ ty re veal ing._____ Ay, ay, ay,

ay,_____ sing, me your sor row.____ To pass the hours____ light ly

sing ing, cie____ li to Lin do here's____ to to mor row._____

A Marine sergeant plays "Taps" during a ceremony in Quantico, Virginia.

Taps

Red River Valley

Cowboy

Little Brown Jug

Traditional

Trumpet in B♭

My wife and I lived all a - lone in a lit - tle log hut we

called our own. She love gin, and I loved rum. I tell you we had

lots of fun. Ha, ha, ha, you and me, lit - tle brown jug, don't

I love thee. Ha, ha, ha, you and me, lit - tle brown jug, don't I love thee.

Did You Know?

The song "Little Brown Jug" was written in 1869. It became nationally popular when Glenn Miller's instrumental version hit the music charts in 1939.

On Top of Old Smokey

American folk song

On top of old Smok ey, all cov ered with snow, _____

— I lost my true lov er by court in' too slow.

Playing the high notes, exercise 1

Playing the high notes, exercise 2

Playing the high notes, exercise 3

Playing the high notes, exercise 4

Playing the high notes, exercise 5

APPENDIX: Finding the Notes

Regardless of which instrument a student of music is learning, a diagram of the keys of the piano offers one of the best illustrations of how most western music is organized. Comprehending the relationship between different notes gives a trumpeter both a greater understanding of his or her instrument and a grasp of the basics of music theory.

Typically, a modern piano has around 88 keys. As you can see in the diagram on the opposite page, these keys are colored either black or white and repeat a specific pattern throughout the keyboard. That is, with the exception of the extreme left of the keyboard (the lowest notes) and the extreme right (the highest notes), you will find groupings of three white keys with two black keys between them and four white keys with three black keys between them. Each of these keys is given a name corresponding to the letters of the alphabet A through G. The letter names are assigned to the white, and the black keys' names are letters with either a sharp sign or flat sign after them.

The pitch that sounds when you strike the white key immediately to the left of the grouping of two black keys is known as C. Depending upon the number of keys on the piano being played, this note will reoccur six or seven times throughout the instrument. The frequency of each C is twice that of the C immediately to its left and one-half that of the C to its right. Because of this special relationship, these notes sound very similar to our ears, hence, the reason why they have the same name. The interval between these adjacent pitches with the same name is known as an octave, and this relationship is true for all similarly named notes found on the keyboard.

In order to clear up confusion caused by the fact that there are as many as 88 notes (maybe more) on a piano and many fewer note names, musicians, over time, have developed a way to differentiate between the notes that have the same name. Beginning with the C note found farthest to the left of the keyboard, a number is added to the note name indicating the octave in which the note occurs. For example, the first C that appears on the

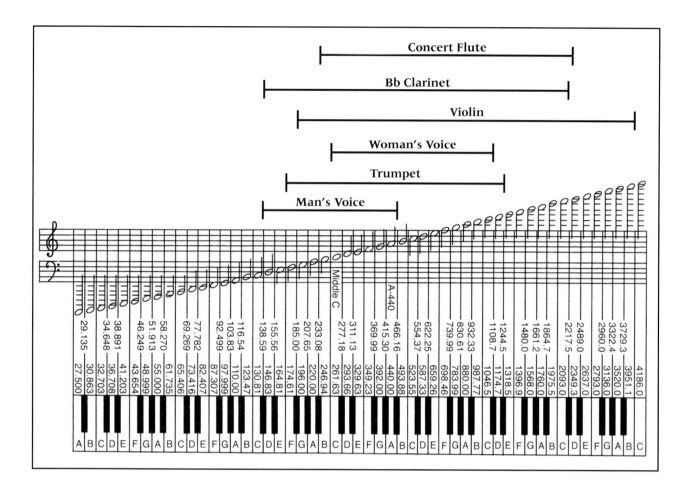

keyboard is known as "C1," the D that appears next to that is known as "D1," and so on. Middle C is also known as C4. Depending upon the piano's manufacturer, you may find that there is a different number of notes to the left of the first C on the keyboard. Since these notes do not comprise a complete octave, the number zero follows their letter name.

You'll notice that there are eleven keys between notes of the same name. Each of these keys represents a change in pitch of one half step. It can then be concluded that an octave covers a distance of 12 half steps, or six whole steps.

APPENDIX: FINGERING CHART

TRUMPET TIMELINE

Prehistory: Primitive trumpets made of hollow branches, bones, animal horns, shells, and plant stems were used by Stone Age humans. Archaeologists believe they had a variety of uses, such as frightening evil spirits or enemies and signaling others. Examples of these instruments still in use today include the *dijeridu* of the Australian aboriginal tribes and conch shells in the South Pacific.

by 380 B.C.: Ancient Egyptians develop a metal trumpet for use in ceremonies and military organization. Trumpets are depicted in King Tutankhamun's tomb. The Chinese, Israelites, Greeks, Tibetans, and Romans are also noted as having used trumpets during this time.

A.D. 1400s: Instrument makers find a way to fold the trumpet, so that it takes on a compact size.

1544: The British army develops specific bugle calls for movements during battle.

1550s: Trumpets with different pipe configurations become parts of orchestras. Multiple trumpet players were needed to cover the full range of notes.

Early 1600s: European trumpeters form the Trompeterkameradschaft, a professional union. Around this time, the instrument is known as the natural trumpet because it has no valves, slides, or pistons. Identified as "clarion" playing, it reaches its peak in the works of Bach and Handel.

Late 1700s: Johann Nepomuk Hummel and Franz Joseph Haydn write music for the keyed trumpet. The trumpet becomes a regular part of the orchestra; crooks (short pieces of coiled brass tubing) were invented and were used to lengthen or shorten the trumpet so it could be used to play more notes.

1788:   Charles Clogget invents the first trumpet valve.

1790s: The United States Congress authorizes one trumpeter to each unit in its cavalry.

1801:   Anton Widinger of Vienna improves the trumpet by adding five keys to it, enabling him to play the chromatic scale.

1814:   Trumpet valves are improved by Heinrich Stolzel, making crooks unnecessary. There are two types of valves created for trumpets: piston valves, which are common in the United States, and rotary valves, like those found on the French horn.

1855:   The cornet is invented in France by Antoine Courtois. He used a mostly conical bore, starting very narrow at the mouthpiece and gradually widening towards the bell, which is unlike the trumpet's mostly cylindrical bore.

1877:   Trumpeter Charles "Buddy" Bolden (d. 1931), the first prominent New Orleans jazz musician, is born. Sometimes known as "King Bolden," he is credited with developing the music that would later become known as jazz between 1895 and 1907. (The word "jazz" would not be commonly used until the 1920s). Bolden influenced many later jazz trumpeters, including Joe "King" Oliver and Louis Armstrong.

1901:   Louis Armstrong (d. 1971), one of the most influential figures in jazz history, is born in New Orleans. A virtuosic trumpeter known for his improvisation skills, many also credit Armstrong with inventing jazz singing. Armstrong's nickname "Satchmo" (or "Satch") is short for "Satchelmouth," a term jokingly coined to describe his embouchure.

1917:   Dizzy Gillespie (d. 1993) is born in South Carolina. Gillespie was a major figure in the development of bebop and modern jazz and is recognized as a founder of Afro-Cuban Jazz. His trademark trumpet, which had a bent bell, was initially the result of an accident. He liked the tone so much that he played with it that way for the rest of his career. (The photo of Gillespie was taken in 1955.)

1926:   Miles Davis (d. 1991), who would become one of the most distinguished jazz musicians of the 20th century, is born on May 26 in Illinois. Davis, a trumpeter, bandleader, and composer, had a hand in nearly every major jazz innovation from the 1940s to the 1990s, and his popularity helped jazz become widely accepted as music with lasting artistic value.

1937:   Harry James joins Benny Goodman's orchestra. James (1916–1983) was known for his immense talent as a trumpeter. When James started his own big band in 1939, he proved to have an eye for talent; among the musicians hired was a then-unknown young vocalist named Frank Sinatra.

1940s: Roy Eldridge (1911–1989), a dynamic trumpeter who could play with sophisticated harmony, is a leading figure during the Swing era. Eldridge played with Gene Krupa, Artie Shaw, Benny Goodman, Count Basie, and Coleman Hawkins; he also recorded solo albums.

1970:   Miles Davis releases the seminal jazz-fusion album *Bitches Brew*, one of the genre's most influential records.

1974:   Trumpeter Quincy Jones suffers a near-fatal cerebral aneurysm, requiring serious brain surgery to save his life. He is told never to play the instrument again, as the pressure required to blow into the trumpet could cause the aneurysm to burst again. Before this incident, Jones had a very successful career as an arranger and composer as well as a musician; he has gone on to become one of the most important figures in the entertainment world, earning more than 70 Grammy Award nominations.

1997:   Bandleader Maynard Ferguson is inducted into the Canadian Music Hall of Fame. Ferguson was a renowned trumpet player known for his ability to play in an extremely high register. Ferguson died in August 2006.

2005:   American trumpeter and composer Wynton Marsalis (b. 1961) receives the National Medal of Arts. A well-known trumpet player, in 1997 Marsalis became the first jazz musician to win a Pulitzer Prize in music. He currently serves as artistic director for Jazz at Lincoln Center in New York City.

2006:   Miles Davis is inducted into the Rock 'n Roll Hall of Fame. Although Davis never played rock or R&B, his forward-thinking sensibility and interest in moving music into unexplored territory appealed to fans of rock and influenced numerous rock musicians, including Duane Allman and Jerry Garcia.

INTERNET RESOURCES

http://musiced.about.com/od/buyingguide/qt/buytrumpet.htm

At this website you'll find a list of helpful tips for buying your first trumpet.

http://www.trumpetherald.com/

This forum is geared towards trumpet players of all ages and skill levels, regardless of playing style. Registration is free and the forums cover subjects from performance and equipment to pedagogy and what schools have the best programs for study.

http://www.trumpetmaster.com/

Here you can find trumpet-related employment. You can also buy and sell trumpets and trumpet accessories, and even speak with artists-in-residence, including Manny Laureano, Wilmer Wise, Ed Carroll, and Tony Kadleck.

http://www.8notes.com/

A great resource for all musicians, this site has trumpet sheet music for 30 songs available for free download, along with fingering charts, a music terms glossary, a free online metronome, and links to other useful music websites.

http://www.hakanhardenberger.com/

Håkan Hardenberger is a trumpet virtuoso and one of the greatest living classically trained trumpeters alive. At his official site you can find excerpts from his recordings, a biography, and performance information.

http://www.ibreathemusic.com/

An invaluable resource for any musician, this site has forums and articles covering a wide range of music-related topics, including composition, improvisation, and ear training.

http://www.zacharymusic.com/Zachary_Music/TRcarePics.htm

Here you'll see a highly informative article describing, in detail, how to care for your trumpet. High quality color photos illustrate each step of the process.

http://www.satchmo.net/

This is the official website of the Louis Armstrong House and Archives, whose mission is to preserve and promote the cultural legacy of one of the greatest trumpeters/vocalists ever.

http://www.milesdavis.com/

Official website of Miles Davis' estate. It contains information about his music, his art, forums about the different periods of his career, and biographical information.

http://www.maynardferguson.com

This is the official website of legendary jazz bandleader and trumpeter Maynard Ferguson.

http://www.wyntonmarsalis.com/

At this website you'll find an abundance of information about one of America's most prominent jazz and classical trumpeter/composers, Wynton Marsalis.

http://www.quincyjonesmusic.com/

His official website, which includes his biography, selected songs, and lyrics along with his catalog.

http://www.menc.org/

The National Association for Music Education is an organization whose mission is to "advance music education by encouraging the study and making of music by all." Go to this site for more information and articles related to issues in music education, making a donation, and becoming a member.

GLOSSARY

Bar lines—these vertical lines mark the division between measures of music.

Beat—the pulse of the music, which is usually implied using the combination of accented and unaccented notes throughout the composition.

Chord—three or more different tones played at the same time.

Clef (bass and treble)—located on the left side of each line of music, these symbols indicate the names and pitch of the notes corresponding to their lines and spaces.

Eighth note—a note with a solid oval, a stem, and a single tail that has 1/8 the value of a whole note.

Embouchure—the adjustment of the lips and tongue in playing a brass instrument.

Flat sign (b)—a symbol that indicates that the note following it should be lowered by one half step. This remains in effect for an entire measure, unless otherwise indicated by a natural sign.

Half note—a note with a hollow oval and stem that has 1/2 the value of a whole note.

Half step—a unit of measurement in music that is the smallest distance between two notes, either ascending or descending. An octave is divided equally into 12 half steps.

Interval—the distance in pitch between two tones, indicated using half and whole steps.

Key signature—found between the clef and time signature, it describes which notes to play with sharps or flats throughout a piece of music.

Measure—a unit of music contained between two adjacent bar lines.

Music staff—the horizontal lines and spaces between and upon which music is written.

Natural sign—a symbol which instructs that a note should not be played as a sharp or a flat.

Notes—written or printed symbols which represent the frequency and duration of tones contained in a piece of music.

Octave—a relationship between two pitches where one tone has double (or half) the frequency of the other.

Pitch—the perceived highness or lowness of a sound or tone.

Quarter note—a note with a solid oval and a stem that is played for 1/4 of the duration of a whole note.

Repeat sign—a pair of vertical dots that appear near bar lines that indicate a section of music that is to be played more than once.

Rest—a figure that is used to denote silence for a given duration in a piece of music.

Scale—a sequence of notes in order of pitch in ascending or descending order.

Sharp sign (#)—this symbol indicates that the note following it should be raised by one half-step. This remains in effect for an entire measure, unless otherwise indicated by a natural sign.

Tempo—the speed at which music is to be played. It is notated by either a word describing the relative speed of the piece or by the number of beats per minute (B.P.M.) that occur as it is played.

Time signature—located to the right of the clef and key signatures, the top digit indicates the number of beats per measure, and the number at the bottom shows which kind of note receives one beat.

Tone—a distinct musical sound which can be produced by a voice or instrument.

Whole note—a note indicated by a hollow oval without a stem. It has the longest time value and represents a length of 4 beats when written in 4/4 time.

Whole step—a unit of measurement in music that is equal to two half steps.

INDEX

ABOUT THE AUTHOR

Frank Cappelli is a warm, engaging artist, who possesses the special ability to transform the simple things of life into a wonderful musical experience. He has had an impressive career since receiving a B.A. in music education from West Chester State College (now West Chester University). Frank has performed his music at many American venues—from Disney World in Florida to Knott's Berry Farm in California—as well as in Ireland, Spain, France, and Italy. He has also performed with the Detroit Symphony, the Buffalo Philharmonic, the Pittsburgh Symphony, and the Chattanooga Symphony.

In 1987, Frank created Peanut Heaven, a record label for children. The following year, he worked with WTAE-TV in Pittsburgh to develop *Cappelli and Company*, an award winning children's television variety show. The weekly program premiered in 1989, and is now internationally syndicated.

In 1989, Frank signed a contract with A&M Records, which released his four albums for children (*Look Both Ways, You Wanna Be a Duck?, On Vacation,* and *Good*) later that year. *Pass the Coconut* was released by A&M in 1991. *Take a Seat* was released in September of 1993. With the 1990 A&M Video release of *All Aboard the Train and Other Favorites* and *Slap Me Five*, Cappelli's popular television program first became available to kids nationwide. Both videos have received high marks from a number of national publications, including *People Magazine, Video Insider, Billboard, USA Today, Entertainment Weekly* and *TV Guide*.

Frank has received many awards, including the Parent's Choice Gold Award, regional Emmy Awards, the Gabriel Award for Outstanding Achievement in Children's Programming, and the Achievement in Children's Television Award. He is a three-time recipient of the Pennsylvania Association of Broadcasters' award for Best Children's Program in Pennsylvania.